MW00873952

Cascade-Siskiyou

poems

Pepper Trail

© 2015 by Pepper Trail

Painted Thrush Press

www.peppertrail.net
ptrail@ashlandnet.net

Cascade-Siskiyou: Poems
ISBN: 9781508484356
First Printing: March 2015

Cover photograph by Pepper Trail

ACKNOWLEDGEMENTS

The following poems appeared in the journals listed below.
I thank the editors for their encouragement and support.

Camas:
"Old Manzanitas"

Cobra Lily:
"The Commerce of the Mountain"
"In an Aspen Grove"

Jefferson Monthly:
"Ponderosa"

Windfall:
"Casualty"
"Ghost"
"Late Riders"
"Logging Show"
"Pond of Newts"

"Madrone Dance" and "Mid-Elevation" were
previously published in *Shifting Patterns: Meditations
on the Meaning of Climate Change in Oregon's Rogue Valley*,
by Pepper Trail and Jim Chamberlain (Blurb, 2009)

Along the Oregon-California border lies a remote and rugged expanse of wild country connecting the Cascade Mountains on the east with the Siskiyou Mountains on the west, and feeding the watersheds of the Rogue River to the north and the Klamath River to the south. To protect the extraordinary diversity of plants and animals found here, the Cascade-Siskiyou National Monument was established by President Clinton in June 2000. All the poems in this collection were written in the monument and its surroundings, at the sites noted after each poem.

These poems are dedicated to Dave Willis, tireless advocate for the establishment, protection, and expansion of the Cascade-Siskiyou National Monument. No place ever had a better friend.

CONTENTS

ECOTONE

Begin with the grass
Not along the road, thatched with medusa
And cheat, but beyond the fenceline, fescue
Rising in sprays of gray-green, uncropped
Tough as wire, made to hold this ground

Upslope and around, southside, sun
Exposes the stones, sets the plants apart
Place of chaparral, where between the brush
The land is clear for flowers
The air bright with butterflies and bees

Then, oaks, the white and the black
Each tree apart, its own world
Season by season, the tender buds
The dark summer shade for rest
In fall, the valley's feasting-place

And always above, the rim
Dark line of trees, from the grassland
To the woodland, forest at the last
Holding the wind and the snow
Hiding the trillium and the owl

Not water alone does flow, but land
All its coverings and its inhabitants
The deer walking from valley to ridge
The birds and the every living thing
Find here, in a world of change, their place

Sampson Creek

HUNTING MORELS

Every spring I hunt morels
Every spring I return empty-handed
Or, perhaps, with one or two, a teasing taste

It is not me, exactly (I tell myself)
I have sharp enough eyes, and in company
Have often spied the mushroom that others missed

But on my hunt the morels elude me
Even as they lead me to look slowly and with care
At the carpet unrolled across the forest floor

To see the heliotrope unfurling in the sun
Frozen explosion of lime-green leaves
The fairy orchids' weightless blooms
Floating above the pillowed moss
The intricate stitchery of bedstraw
Tying tight the leaf-strewn tapestry

To do what I love
To fail utterly
To return home satisfied
That is why I hunt morels

Soda Mountain

OLD MANZANITAS

I love them for their complications of the living
    and the dead
Their inner wood, breaking out on every twisting limb
The weathered grain exposed in long gray creases
Encrusted with lichen, pale green and ashen
And hung with the dank black tufts of witch's beard
I love how that disagrees with the smooth and molded skin
Running in ribbons, color of ox-blood, of brick and
    deep red earth
I love the coin-shaped leaves, offered in trembling
Hands to the cold spring wind
I love the flowers, tiny shell-like urns
Rounded and pink as a sleeping baby's toes
First food for the returning hummingbirds
Who feast upon the nectar, flashing copper and gold
And most, perhaps, I love their shapes upon the
    mountainside
In stillness, crouching, spinning, reaching, sprawling,
    dancing
Their endurance, their squat and knotted selves
Their refusal to resemble one another, or any other
    living thing
Their difference, and their difficulty, and their grace

Upper Emigrant Creek

13

POND OF NEWTS

Snow still beneath the dark firs
And from there the melt into the meadow's sponge
The drawing down until joined as freshet
To babble and gush into the pond of newts

In that ice water, cold-blooded, cold-eyed
The newts abide, awake and in need
Of all that we all need: air that must be
Purchased at the surface, a tedious routine
Food that must be found in the silty mud
Lust that must be slaked, by seizing or being seized

Rough-skinned but soft, flat heads full of mouth
Tall tails pinched thin, they seem created
By a child god, an early, imperfect miracle
Set free to find their way as best they can
But not left defenseless; at the last moment
Lifted up, their bellies washed with poison stain

So, attacked, they offer not defense but demonstration
Curving the body back, writhing the tail
Flashing orange as toxins seep from skin
Signaling sickness to the wise
Giving to the greedy, death

Porcupine Meadows

SHORT HIKE

I did not get far.
From the trailhead, I walked perhaps
a hundred yards, and there appeared
a slope crowded with naked, dancing oaks,
and I climbed to join them, sat sunwarmed
to watch, and at my feet were scattered flowers,
buttercups and larkspurs, *Senecio* and saxifrage,
and across the valley the hills fell
from gray-green summits to emerald
along the creek, and from the Doug-fir snag
the flicker laughed and laughed,
and there I spent my day.

Upper Emigrant Creek

FIRE ECOLOGY

My hope is that we burn cold
The best to be hoped for is that we do not consume all
That more than ash remains after our passing
I mean, after this burn and before the next
Recurrence being the law

Drive the auger into the bole, hand over hand
Clockwise, against the fight of the grain, the squeak of the wood
Draw out the core with care, read there
Black lines among the blond rings, scars that tell other stories
The year of the drought, the year of the broken heart
That death, and this one here, and this one
The finger tracing, father, sister, friend
Black rims building beneath fingernails
At each footfall, gray dust rising

Fire will come
Let it not be wild, let something remain
Seeds, children, streams in their beds
And here and there, lonely but alive
The great old, speaking to the wind

Grizzly Peak

THE COMMERCE OF THE MOUNTAIN

The bumblebee, squat and hairy bagman, trundles around his neighborhood, one flower to the nearby next, filling his sacks with gold, humming to himself all the while. On a fine August day, there is no more self-satisfied citizen on the mountain.

The warblers are in motley now, their badges of black and yellow worn to tatters, the dramas of song, courtship, nest and eggs and hungry mouths forgotten, mingling in the ragamuffin democracy of migration, nothing left to fight for and enough for all.

The hummingbird harbors still his zest for rage, his blood hot, his pride easily pricked, his honor forever to be defended. Lord of his patch of penstemon, he is on the dash, looking for trouble, flashing his sword, seeking a challenger, exulting in heat, and sugar, and speed.

Overhead, the vulture walks the tightrope of sky, balances on dark wings, ignorant of flowers, disinterested in bumblebees, hummingbirds, warblers, all too small in death to reach him with news of their decay, blind to the bright, with no taste for the sweet, meadowless and alone.

Pilot Rock

CHANT

Deep in the April woods
The grouse moans forth his chant
It passes untouched
Between the great trunks
And through the fine needles
Travels across the ravines
And over the ridges
Sets my breastbone buzzing
Rings the bell that is my beating heart

Upper Emigrant Creek

SUCCULENCE

A misstep among the rocks, worn sole
Skidding on the patch of stonecrop
Swollen leafpads torn, the hoarded water
A spilled smear of glue

I stumble and sit to avoid the fall, steady
My breath, reach a finger to the sticky
Sap, bring it to my tongue, taste
The bitter and the cool

I busy myself, open my heavy book
Begin to parse and key, work down
To *Sedum*, then to *obtusatum* perhaps
But certainty needs a flower

In the end, I go on uninjured

This moment returns to me in transit
Standing in that desolation of travel
Before the great white windows
In (the sign says) Denver

In the heat, it is hard
To stay soft; in the dry, wet
Against the wind, rooted
Through the years, green

I remember now that I asked no pardon
Of the broken plant, gave no thanks
There on the cliff's edge
For its blood and its name

So here, outcast, I do

Porcupine Mountain

19

FALSE HELLEBORE

Noble and tall, richly flowered
Filling the mountain swales
With towers of bloom
Great lily, how rude we are
To weigh you down
With the name of our confusion
There is nothing false in you
True you are to your nameless nature

And what of hellebore, true hellebore
Saddled now with this untrue, unknown twin
It is a mercy that flowers live their lives
Beyond the reach of our taxonomy

So as we fumble the world into order
We label, segregate, and confuse
Spread upon each leaf and blossom
A sparkling dust of words, visible
To our burning eyes alone

Porcupine Meadows

FRESHET

The tendriled stream
    finds its way over the flat brown grasses
carries the meltwater, clear as air
        from the blue shadowed snowbanks
across the meadow, delivers it with swirl
      and gurgle into the larger creek, fenced by willows
already blurred with soft white buds
    and soon, the willows in leaf, the world
      returned to green, this first stream, source
of awakening, will be gone
    unless, dazed with spring
you blunder off the trail
      to find the freshet hiding
        waiting for your boots

Hyatt Lake

ODE TO BUCKBRUSH

Ghost-green scrub of the valleysides
How well-schooled you are in difficulty!
Each piece of you a masterpiece of exclusion
Your branches interlocked, short and stiff
Jagged palisade of leaf-bearing thorns
The starving winter deer may prune you
But you remain complete

As you obstruct the great, you shelter the small
In the summer season, the towhees and the wrens
Find safety for eggs and the needy young
Within the sanctuary of your prickly heart
The woodrat builds his lodge, and hoards
His treasury of stolen things, snakeskins and shell casings
Here the sparrows spend their long and fearful nights

Come spring, you blossom white
Your dry and crumbling blooms fill the air
With dusty scent of summer's impending heat
Driving mad the bees and the black-haired flies
Who drag themselves through your pollen
Drunk upon this first abundance
Of the reawakened earth

And what of fire, predator of all that grows?
On these sun-struck slopes, of course you burn
Your flesh is fuel like all the rest
But you are made to flare hot and fast
Surrender your body to pass the fire
Quickly on, so to save something
From the recurrent apocalypse

In the stony ground, broken by your roots
Your seeds lie in their thousands, sleeping
To be awakened by the scorch of passing flames
Cracking their coats, freeing their sprouts
Into a world new, fertilized by ash
Purified by fire, ready to grow again
Ghost-green, covered with buckbrush, you

Horseshoe Wildlife Area

THE GIFT OF SIGHT

Begin with landscape, the eastern slopes
Pale stacked cliffs before us
The green mountains behind, unrevealing

Habitations replacing plains, roads encircling
Creeks concealing rivers, low gray clouds the sky

Dreaming, my eyes are closed
       In this circle where we sit, the gift of sight
       Passed around, hand to hand, reaches me
       Impatient, I pass it on

The sun rises above the ridge
I feel it on my face, less cold
Behind my eyes, less dark

We get to our feet, all
Turn as one, steady, stand
Facing together, like flowers
The unseen dawn

Hobart Bluff

24

STREWN

This garden is not planted, but strewn,
the gardener industrious as wind,
throwing pollen in handfuls of gust,
assigning to each berry, a bird,
to each seed, an ant, to carry
to the precise, unplanned, and
prepared place of germination.

And so, scattered through the grass
beneath the greening oaks, are swaths
of bloom, blue-eyed mary and
prairie stars, the dusky downy
cups of pussy's ears, the ardent yellow
spires of butterwort, the larkspurs,
their purple so deep our vision is held
quiet and still, tranquilized by beauty.

This particular, particulate harmony
is nature's random own, beyond our
most diligent work and care but
ever-returning, needing from us
only to be free.

Upper Emigrant Creek

THE COLUMBINE

Vertical beneath the columbine
The hummingbird twirls, suspended
Precisely probes
One, two, three, four, five
Drops of nectar taken
And is gone
Leaving the nodding flower
Satisfied

Soda Mountain

SNAIL

Snail, I see you through the water's lens
Wet as I am dry, cool as I am hot
Inhabitant of another world, three feet away
We sit upon the same rock, mine rough and grey
Yours smooth and green to the waterline
A pasture of sweet algae for you to graze upon

Single-footed steer with a speckled shell
In your limpid pool, murmuring and never still
There are troubles enough, I know
Just as here, in the stirring, sound-filled air
But you, fitted at birth with everything you have
You do not find cause to think or worry

While I, somehow, I do

Jenny Creek

THE BULL

Across the mountain slope
Over the wildflower meadows
Through the lichen-shrouded trees
Into the grove where I sit

Comes the bellow of a bull
Mindless monosyllabic roar
The cry of the consumer
Unleashed, ascendant

For the long breath of each roar
The music of the forest is lost
The thrush's song, the junco's trill
Near and far, all drowned

All part of a harmony
That has no place for the bull
That the bull is here to eat
And then, be eaten

Soda Mountain

ALARMS

Entering the forest I find
It is filled with alarms, shrill
Sharp calls of woodpeckers
Brittle chips of sparrows
The jeers of jays, furious
Trills of squirrels, vibrating
With warning and scorn
All this rage and fear
Just for me, my noisy boots
My pale legs protruding from
Ragged shorts, my binoculars
My notebook, my earnest watchful
Face, for that other world
That I am

I sit on a rock and write this down, and the forest relaxes
back into itself. As I am about to rise, I hear approaching
calls not of alarm, but of conversation, the companionable
back and forth of comrades or of a family, and over the
nearby log four quail appear, walking and talking at their
ease. Twenty feet away they spot my strange still shape
and stop. After a long moment, they decide that I am odd,
too odd, and return the way they came, quietly commenting
among themselves on what they have seen, until I can no
longer hear them, and I am left alone in the silent woods.

Pilot Rock

HERO

At my footstep,
the woodpecker flies,
abandons the log.
This time,
the ants are saved.

Pilot Rock

PONDEROSA

The tree is a library, a tight-rolled scroll
Layers of scribbled sheets pressed together
Guarding their truths against rain and fire

Each season, life writes a new report
Records, with incised letters and furrowed lines
Selections from the infinite world of incident

At the foot of the tree, a pile of torn pages
Puzzle-shaped scraps, no two alike
Their traces embossed on the remaining text

Illiterate, I spread my hand upon the bark
Must content myself with the beauty of the book
The magic contained in words unread

                                            Dutch Oven Creek

THE BORDER

There is a river, there is a ridge
A way beyond through rocks and trees
A border there to cross, but first
It must be found, where it lies
Meaningless, invisible, and straight
Running not like water down
Nor quite east or west

It is laid upon the earth and
Also claims the air, claims
The birds as innocent they fly across
Claims the raindrops as they split
Upon that razor edge, and changes
The river's color as it passes by

In this world of solid things
Of wood and stone, rough ground
And green enduring leaves
My fingers reach, reach past the real
Forever seek the border
Crossed, again and again
But never found

Soda Mountain

OLD REELFOOT

I am Old Reelfoot
The last grizzly bear
My right foot is mangled
From the time I learned about traps
My hide holds 20 pounds of lead
From every time you got a shot at me
You poisoned my mother
Shot my father
Killed each of the six cubs that I fathered
Back when there were still mothers
Now for many years I have been alone
Here, upon the ridges

I live well enough upon your cattle
So tender and so dumb
But I am not satisfied
I am no fool
I know you will kill me in the end
Wipe my kind from the face of the earth
And so I look down upon your cabin
Watching, waiting for my chance
To break clear of the brush
To roll over you like an avalanche
To take your head in my jaws
And crack it like a nut

We have good reason to hate, you and I
And I know that I cannot win
But I will never accept you
Never yield to you, never bow
As long as I live, I fight
As long as I live, you have not yet won

Pilot Rock

OPPOSITES

The opposite of May is August
Of the flower, the seed
Of hoping, knowing
Of all that may be
All that there is

Pilot Rock

CASUALTY

– for Seamus Heaney

The old road leads upward,
knobbed and straight
as the spine of a woman's bowed back.
I follow it to the end, reach the furzy oaks
and the longer pines at the crest,
look out and down, north
where the sun leans on its spade,
leaves the cool to settle.
The trees gather here, touch hands,
speak little, do their work,
ask for nothing. Their due is only
to be left in peace,
but this is not a time of peace.

Below, a ripping buzz, speeding,
slowing, speeding, then shouts,
then a crack in the air.
A tree takes a step, stumbles,
slowly falls with crash and echo.

At end of day, I cross broken
ground, stone and bark,
arms full of needles,
but the body gone,
carried off to be worked upon.
The stump remains for me to touch.
The pitch is soft and red.
It will not leave my hand.

Greensprings Mountain

35

HAIKU – SPRING

Across the valley
The bare oaks on the green hills
So much yet to come

Sampson Creek

Sharp magenta darts
These flowers called shooting stars
Pierce the heart of spring

Buck Rock

Purple, white, and green
The mountain meadow in May
Snow, in full bloom

Boccard Point

HAIKU – SUMMER

The hummingbird dives
Tears a small hole in the sky
Flies through, and is gone

> Boccard Point

Summer waterfall
Thread of water over rock
In the green canyon

> Dutch Oven Creek

This June evening
You were given perfection
Did you accept?

> Pilot Rock

HAIKU – AUTUMN

On the ridge, the oaks
Offer golden leaves, one by one
To the autumn wind

                                        Jenny Creek

The old dragonfly
Struggles in the yellow reeds
Autumn afternoon

                                        Jenny Creek

As the woods grow dark
The croak of a passing raven
Perfects the silence

                                        Soda Mountain

HAIKU – WINTER

New day and new year
Across the stream, the dry grass
Shivers in the cold

Jenny Creek

A coyote's track
Step into step, numberless
The hungry miles home

Hyatt Lake

A drift of kinglets
Passes, leaves behind only
Sound of falling snow

Pilot Rock

THE MAN ON THE RIDGE

An old man sleeps upon the ridge
Dividing the Klamath from the Rogue
His hard head is Pilot Rock
His arms cradle the creeks
His legs stretch from canyon to plateau
His heart lies at Boccard Point

A man whose ribs are rock
Whose blood is water flowing
Whose skin is soil
Who is clothed in forest

He dreams of sagebrush and of fir
Of lightning strikes and lava flows
Of the trees dancing east and west
Through years of drought and years of rain
Beneath the circling stars

I ride upon the old man's back
Warm my hands against his skin
We do not need to speak
We share the same dreams

Boccard Point

MADRONE DANCE

No tree, standing still , moves as you move
No limbs so bare, so sleek, so suited for the dance
You crouch and stride, balance and curve
Arms aloft, the art of gesture is yours, all yours
And the pines stand around you
Stiff with scandalized admiration

O madrone, dance now, dance
As never, dance up the mountainside
Fast and faster than ever you have done
Use the birds, all of them, the flocking
Robins and the waxwings, the starlings and the thrushes
In these hot days, burst with berries
'Send them far and wide, send them
Always higher, find that place
Wherever it has gone, still cool
But below the hardest cold
Dry, but above the cracking earth

The time has come to run
You, madrone, cannot run
So, dance

Upper Emigrant Creek

41

VARIED THRUSH

Wilder robin, painted thrush
You beam your high unearthly trills
Through the trees and into outer space
Sit, slender-headed, ready to fly
Ever ready to leave the common flock
Your habitat, always, a better place than this

Upper Emigrant Creek

THE BERRY-WOODS

How secret and alive, the berry-woods
All song stilled, the boasting season done
Nothing to be heard but murmurs and calls
Bursts of flutter, birds lost within the leaves
Swallowing the pin-cherries, bright as rubies
The Oregon grapes, hard and full of spice
The manzanitas, their little apples sweet
Today, the world balances dark and light
The agitations of spring long past
Summer's full schedule forgotten
This autumn work is simply gathering
Feasting, growing fat beneath the feathers
Preparing to fly before the cold
Before winter opens its empty hands

Pilot Rock

FOREST VOICES

The jays will not allow
The forest to be silent
Their voices shape the wild
Like yours, like mine

Soda Mountain

RESURRECTION

Shell pink and mint green, the manzanitas
Spread Easter across the April hills
And to them came an ancient, battered,
Buried and resurrected butterfly
To feed and rest upon the blooms
A Mourning Cloak with wings so frayed
That only the ghosts of their finery remained

Survivor of what cold and bitter crypt
The stone now rolled from the door
The lost one returned to the world
Bearing the burden for which it all was done
Her body swollen with the promise fulfilled
The eggs that bring life everlasting
Before this miracle, I kneel.

Upper Emigrant Creek

HUMMINGBIRD

Sharpening knife of song
On stone of sky
The hummingbird, keen
For each instant of passing life
Engages the world in constant duel
Gorget of glittering red
Throat already cut
Perfectly alive

Soda Mountain

VINEGARWEED

In August the sun strikes the south-
Facing slopes on the mountainside
And lifts into the air a strange perfume
Not sweet and light, not drifting from flowers
For the enticement of honeybees
But oily, viscid and spicy
Wrung by the sun from leathery leaves
A nose-twisting scent, strong and strange
A scent that wakes me from the late-summer slumber
Clears my head, reminds me just in time
Of the shortening days, the approaching frost
The end, at last, of dull-witted ease

Hobart Bluff

TO A YOUNG LIZARD

It is September now
The sun strikes warm still
On the flat back of this mountain ridge
But the light is moving away
And every night grows strangely colder
All this is new in your life, summer-born
Is there room in your imagination
For what winter is, the long dangerous sleep
Or is it just a blank white cold?

Whether this or that, the time has come
To hunt, to feed and feed until
Soft with fat, stiff with sleep
You wedge your way, deep and deeper
Down a jagged fractal crack
There to wait and all but die
Until the sun of another year returns
To melt the snow and warm the rock
To return, somehow, warmth and life to you
To bring you back to stand upon your stone
Alive and ignorant and wise

Hobart Bluff

LOGGING SHOW

Standing at the edge of last week's logging show,
on the scraped red earth, before the house-high piles of
    slash,
I do not admire, even a little, those storied men,
the log-buckers, Cat-drivers, choker-setters
who populate our Oregon mythology,
who make their living "in the woods,"
and are said to love them.

Love them, as with practiced eyes and all the machines
they need, they pull them down, wreck them, and then
drive away from the broken mess,
the few standing trees barked and bleeding,
the crushed soil fit only for mullein and thistle,
the forest broken, unmendable as an egg.

All this for a few big trees that could have been
eased out of the woods with a little more time
and thought and care, but with, perhaps, a little
less profit and certainly much less show,
less grease and smoke and roughneck mythology,
less of all that is somehow called honest work.

Copco Road
(industrial timberland
adjacent to the monument)

MOUNTAIN MAHOGANY

August lights candleflames
In this darkest of trees
Glowing silver seeds
Twisting in the constant wind
Sparks, ready to fly

Hobart Bluff

GHOST

Halfway up the ridge
Heart painful in my chest
I stopped in a juniper's twisted shade
Ancient and broken, the tree still bore
Life in its limbs, the twigs green-scaled
And at work in the sun
The berries filmed with
Strange ghost-blue bloom

Unsummoned, the ghost was there
My closest dead, my father
Eyes of that blue, then
Dimming to the old brown
He looked at me silent
Perhaps surprised but seeming
Not displeased to be here conjured
Upon the wild mountainside

Only the one look, then fading
And gone into thinning air
But such looks were his native tongue
This one spoke of his accommodation
To where he had gone, his quiet satisfaction
To have this brief sight of me
It was one with the instructions
And the rewards of my childhood

Alone, I reached out my hand
Picked one fruit of the juniper
The blue vanished at my touch
I crushed the bruised berry in my teeth
It was hard, bitter, resinous, inedible
Not food but spice
Flavor of loss
Ingredient of remembering

Hobart Bluff

GRASSHOPPER

The brown grasshopper
Dust-colored, bullet-headed
Takes flight
Spreads yellow wings
Above the broken stones
For that moment
A butterfly

Hobart Bluff

ALONE UNDER THE SUN

It is no difficult thing, to be alone among the trees
Between their heavy boles, shadowed by drooping limbs
It is easy to hide by standing still
Easy to find a narrow solitude

But how rare is this empty valley
Folded between the stone-faced hills
The trees standing at a respectful distance
The broad green meadows full only of water-silence

This is where I come to be alone beneath the sun
Sole inhabitant, for that time, of a whole home range
Advance scout into an unpeopled land
Explorer back into a lost, lost world

Jenny Creek

WHAT IT TAKES

It takes one eagle
To fill the sky

Two eagles to bless this valley
As wild

Buck Point

THE MOLTING SEASON

August, and the forest is full of feathers
Here, dropped by a jay, still so blue
And farther, grouse, a dappled covert
To hide in, but in my hand
A tapestry revealed
Intricate, astonishing
And last, a pinion
Lost from a hawk's wing
White and brown, shaped to cut the air
A knife, fallen at my feet

This is the molting season, fledglings flown
The pair bond loosened or lost
Now is the time to fly toward freedom
On ragged wings

Jenny Creek

IN AN ASPEN GROVE

Here I was born, October, my month
Season of fruition and the fall
Beginning from here, I grew
In some ways changed, but always
Remained and am, now, on this rock
One

One body, one mind despite its disarray
One set of legs that pull me through
The world, one pair of hands to grasp
And feed my one hungry mouth
How strange to be, within these trees
Alone

The aspens are a multitude, each
A clone, the grove an acre of organism
Most living, some few dead, broken and rotting
Feeding the colony that lives, sends roots
Into the soft fallen bodies that thus regain
The many

Above my head, the leaves, particulates of light
Forever tremble, shiver the blue sky to shards
Golden and golden green, each limb hundreds
Each tree thousands, each gust sending more
West across the meadow, burning, then quenched
In shadow

And with the light, the sound, ceaseless
Rustle and murmuration, the bare white
Noise of wind tuned by turning leaves
To sense, to conversation, to the hubbub
Of a community conversing
In harmony

O, how lonely it is to be
In the aspen grove, dark beneath
Those golden leaves, speechless
Within that confabulation, needing
Everything, and always only
One

Soda Mountain

NATURAL FOODS

Here and there in the dirt on the ridge
Are small hollows, made by small hands
In each, the papery skins of bulbs, rosy and white
While from rock to rock to rock
Dart chipmunks
With painted pointed faces
Onions on their breath

Soda Mountain

ANOTHER POINT OF VIEW

Invisible in the shadow beneath the jutting ledge
The cougar reclines and gazes down the rocky slope
At an impossible fool who wanders
Stopping and starting, along the dusty path

Now lifting binoculars, now rummaging in his bag
Now peering at a flower, now reading, now writing
Never looking behind, never scenting the breeze
Never showing the least respect, the slightest care

So slow and so soft, a great baby alone in the wild
Or old, and lost in the dimness before death, perhaps
Too easy a meal, alarmingly aimless
Not for this has the cougar practiced for a million years

Her puff of breath disturbs the dust
And she closes her eyes, dissatisfied
While I, a hundred yards below
Begin to think about having lunch

                                        Lower Scotch Creek

MARDON SKIPPER

We have come here for you,
Small orange blur among the wildflowers
So easily confused with those other butterflies
The Woodland Skipper, the Sandhill, the Sonoran
You are rare, and we are worried

With our hearts full of love
We come lumbering out of the trees
Too coarse to do anything that you do:

>   Fly
>   Alight upon a blade of grass
>   Sip the nectar from a violet
>   Know our place in the world

But with our long-handled nets
Our guides and keys, our close-focus binoculars
We are confident that we will find you
That our witness will make you real
And that, real, you will be, somehow, safe

Soda Mountain

LATE RIDERS

Time misjudged, we watch the sun leave us
Behind the rounded shoulder of the butte
And heel our horses into a fleeting trot, which soon
Returns to the steady gait they know is best

The sky holds light awhile, but not the earth
The grass goes sullen from gold to dun, shivering
Trees shed their bulk, stiffen into silhouettes
Signaling warning and possession

At our approach, deer flow uphill between the pines
Fleeing patches of darkness, into greater darkness
Beyond the caravan sounds of horses and riders
The valley rings with silence

Before full night, there will be a house, a lighted door
But for now, we ride into gray, the falling cold
Speechless, reliant on our mounts
Every moment, more invisible

                                        Horseshoe Wildlife Area

BODHISATTVA

Pine of the mountain forest
For centuries you were the world
For the fleeting beings
The fungi, insects, and birds
Who lived upon you

For decades you stood as a snag
As the ants made within you
A city, doomed to be destroyed
By woodpeckers, wildly crying
As they worked their destruction

Finally you fell, and for long years
You have been melting into the soil
Until today, scattered rusty bits of wood
Strewn across your mounded, fertile grave
Are the last sign of your long and blessed life

Bodhisattva

Grizzly Peak

MID-ELEVATION

Above the valley oaks and the madrones
That stir the lower woods with their naked curves
Higher up, a special feeling comes
The feeling of the mountain, awakening
Cool water for my dull and drowsy face

Here the old trees hold back the falling land
Rise up from a simple ground, fallen limbs and stones
And here modest flowers show themselves
Yellow violets small as sparks, the last deer flowers
Fading with the snow, and trilliums, stars in that dark

The trees speak patience, in the ceaseless murmuration
Of their needles, in their very rootedness, their gravity
Beyond that constant breath, there is little sound
But at length the hermit thrush sings alone
Lovely and slow, comfortable in his invisibility

Through the long day, the shadows circle every tree
Rain may fall, or perhaps the last snow melts
A fire may burn, and seem to mark an end
But we do not know the time these mountains know
Here what has been, will be again

Baldy Creek

THE GLADE

Too many and various
The autumn glade too rich for haiku or maybe
Words
The thimbleberry leaves fat and green along the creek
Going golden, then tan higher up the slope
White snowberries bending down their bushes
Then hazel, then maple
One dogwood half gone salmon-red
Spreading over a deer trail
Two Douglas-fir lean together
Above all
And a square granite boulder
Hooded with moss
Anchors the whole

But that is only
Sight
There is the slanting sweet
And earthy scent
Of fall
The bursts of notes and the
Snap of wings
As juncos thrust and feint
Beneath the big leaves
The whoop and giggle
Of a quail alarmed at
The sound of her own
Footsteps
And from high in the air
As pure and distant as heaven
The kinglets' calls drift down
To rest in the forest
Garden

Upper Emigrant Creek

64

JUNIPER YEARS

The juniper on the ridgeline
Flows horizontally before the wind
Wood hard as iron
Fluid as a wave

It has lived each of its days
Ever in drought, ever hot or cold
Ever pushed by the wind
Ever pushing back

I cannot reckon the juniper's age
Because I cannot live a juniper year
Cannot imagine the endurance
Contained in a single juniper day

But in its stoic grace
Its distillation of the ridge, the wind
The juniper, old and young, green and gray
Teaches that life and time are one

This ant at my feet, this juniper, and myself
We all live the same number of days
All enter and leave the world alike
And are given the time between

Time enough to accomplish our own perfection
To grow, to express in the shape of our lives
The beauty of our afflictions
The worth of all the time there is

Scotch Creek Ridge

BIOGRAPHY

Pepper Trail has lived in southern Oregon for twenty years, and is a leading voice for the protection of the wild and remote Cascade-Siskiyou region. His poetry has appeared in *Windfall, Atlanta Review, Borderlands,* and *Cascadia Review,* among other publications, and has been nominated for Pushcart and Best of the Net awards. He lives in Ashland, Oregon, where he works for the U.S. Fish and Wildlife Service. In 2013 he was honored as the poet laureate of the Cascade-Siskiyou National Monument.

54047927R00043

Made in the USA
Charleston, SC
24 March 2016